HOL

HOLY DAYS

Meditations on the Feasts, Fasts, and Other Solemnities of the Church

Pope Benedict XVI

• •

Edited and Annotated by
JEAN-MICHEL COULET

Introduction and Annotations Translated by
D. C. SCHINDLER

A Giniger Book
published in association with

WILLIAM B. EERDMANS PUBLISHING COMPANY
GRAND RAPIDS, MICHIGAN / CAMBRIDGE, U.K.

Published 2012 by
Wm. B. Eerdmans Publishing Co.
2140 Oak Industrial Drive N.E., Grand Rapids, Michigan 49505 /
P.O. Box 163, Cambridge CB3 9PU U.K.
www.eerdmans.com

Published in association with
The K. S. Giniger Company
1045 Park Avenue, New York, NY 10028

Printed in the United States of America

17 16 15 14 13 12   7 6 5 4 3 2 1

Library of Congress Cataloging-in-Publication Data

Benedict XVI, Pope, 1927-
Holy days: meditations on the feasts, fasts, and other solemnities of the church /
Pope Benedict XVI; edited and annotated by Jean-Michel Coulet;
introduction and annotations translated by D. C. Schindler.

p.   cm.
"A Giniger book."
ISBN 978-0-8028-6518-2 (pbk.: alk. paper)
1. Fasts and feasts — Catholic Church.   I. Title.

BV43.B43513   2012
242′.3 — dc23

2012013198

Contents

Introduction

For Benedict XVI, "the liturgical year is a great voyage of faith on which the Church sets us out." The feast days in the Church's liturgical calendar give a rhythm to our lives as we pass through the year, a rhythm that follows the major events of Jesus' life as recounted in the Gospels. The presentation of these holy days with Benedict XVI's own words helps us better understand the mystery in which the pope invites us to participate. From the beginning of his pontificate, he has not ceased to show us how to come to know and love the Church, and has led us along the path of holiness. He enables us to touch, with our own hands, the grandeur and beauty of the divine mystery: in his words, "It is Christ himself who is at the heart of the liturgy."

It is important, especially in this secularized age, to rediscover certain practices that form us, practices that guide and deepen our path. We are like laborers who dig ever-deeper furrows in the earth with the plow of our heart, in order that we may grow ever higher. God wishes to renew the world by way of the same path that Christ himself followed. Thus, everything is meant to unfold according to the humble and patient logic of the grain of wheat, which, having fallen to the ground, dies in order to give life.

We have to learn to know and live liturgical time by recalling, again and again, that this time is nourished by a constant relationship between tradition and progress. These two concepts complement each other harmoniously, because tradition is a living reality, and includes within itself the seed of development, of progress. Liturgy is an ensemble of acts, symbols, and words, by means of which the Church, made up of women and men, offers worship to God and hands down the knowledge of God to others. The definitive goal always remains the glory of God and the sanctification of his people.

The meditations on the feast days of the Church that are offered in this little book are excerpts selected from the words pronounced by Pope Benedict XVI over the course of the liturgical year as it is lived in Rome. It begins with Advent and concludes with the feast of Christ the King.

> JEAN-MICHEL COULET
> Editor of the French editions
> of the Vatican newspaper
> *L'Osservatore Romano*

Advent

Advent (derived from the Latin word adventus*) is the time in which we experience the presence of eternity and eagerly await its arrival. For precisely this reason it is in a particular way the time of joy, an interior joy that no suffering can take away. It is joy over the fact that God made himself a child. This joy, which we carry hidden within us, gives us the courage to continue forward into the future with confidence. Present among us, it speaks to us in different ways: in the Holy Scriptures, in the liturgical year, in the saints, in the events of daily life, and in the whole of creation.*

ADVENT

First Vespers of Advent

Everyone knows how important the liturgy is to Pope Benedict XVI. The beginning of the liturgical year thus deserves to be celebrated in a solemn way by a Mass that introduces the people of God into the new year. This celebration takes place in St. Peter's, and follows closely the celebration of Christ the King. The term "advent" can be translated as "presence," "arrival," "coming."

Advent, this powerful liturgical season that we are beginning, invites us to pause in silence to understand a presence. It is an invitation to understand that the individual events of the day are hints that God is giving us, signs of the attention he has for each one of us. How often does God give us a glimpse of his love! To keep, as it were, an "interior journal" of this love would be a beautiful and salutary task for our life! In the language of the ancient world it was a technical term used to indicate the arrival of an official or the visit of the king or emperor to a province. However, it could also mean the coming of the divinity that emerges from concealment to manifest himself forcefully or that was celebrated as being present in worship. Christians used the word "advent" to express their relationship with Jesus Christ: Jesus is the King who entered this poor "province" called "earth" to pay everyone a visit; he makes all those who believe in him participate in his coming, all who believe in his presence in the liturgical assembly. The essential meaning of the word *adventus* was: God is here, he has not withdrawn from the world, he has not deserted us. Even if we cannot see and touch him as we can tangible realities, he is here and comes to visit us in many ways.

First Sunday of Advent

This Sunday, by the grace of God, a new liturgical year opens, of course, with Advent, a season of preparation for the birth of the Lord. The Second Vatican Council, in the Constitution on the Liturgy, affirms that the Church "in the course of the year . . . unfolds the whole mystery of Christ from the Incarnation and Nativity to the Ascension, to Pentecost and the expectation of the blessed hope of the Coming of the Lord." The Council insists on the fact that the center of the liturgy is Christ, around whom the Blessed Virgin

Mary, closest to him, and then the martyrs and the other saints who "sing God's perfect praise in heaven and intercede for us," revolve like the planets around the sun. This is the reality of the liturgical year seen, so to speak, "from God's perspective." And from the perspective, let us say, of humankind, of history and of society, what importance can it have? The answer is suggested to us precisely by the journey through Advent on which we are setting out today. The contemporary world above all needs hope; the developing peoples need it, but so do those that are economically advanced. We are becoming increasingly aware that we are all on one boat and together must save each other. Seeing so much false security collapse, we realize that what we need most is a trustworthy hope. This is found in Christ alone. As the Letter to the Hebrews says, he "is the same yesterday and today and for ever" (Heb. 13:8).

December 8: The Immaculate Conception, the Second Sunday of Advent

According to tradition, the pope comes to the Piazza di Spagna, in Rome, in order to say a prayer at the Virgin's feet.

He entrusts the city and the world to the protection of the Immaculate Conception. Until recently, he also used to go to Santa Maria Maggiore in order to pray before the icon of the "Salus populi Romani" [salvation of the Roman people].

Mary Immaculate helps us to rediscover and to defend the deep interior dimension of persons, because in her the body is perfectly transparent to the soul. She is purity in person. The Virgin teaches us to open ourselves to the action of God so that we may look at others the way he looks at them: from his heart.

What does Mary being "Immaculate" mean? And what does this title tell us? First of all, let us refer to the biblical texts of today's liturgy, especially the great "fresco" of the third chapter of the book of Genesis and the account of the Annunciation in the Gospel according to Luke. After the original sin, God addresses the serpent, which represents Satan, curses it and adds a promise: "I will put enmity between you and the woman, and between your seed and her seed; he shall bruise your head, and you shall bruise his heel" (Gen. 3:15). It is the announcement of revenge: at the dawn of the creation, Satan seems to have the upper hand, but the son of a woman is to crush his head. Thus, through the offspring of a woman, God himself will triumph. Goodness will triumph. That woman is the Virgin Mary of whom was born Jesus Christ who, with his sacrifice, defeated the ancient tempter once and for all. This is why in so many paintings and statues of the Virgin Immaculate she is portrayed in the act of crushing a serpent with her foot. Luke the Evangelist, on the other hand, shows the Virgin Mary receiving the Annunciation of the heavenly Messenger (cf. Luke 1:26-38). She appears as the humble, authentic daughter of Israel, the true Zion in which God wishes to take up his abode. She is the shoot from which the Messiah, the just and merciful king, is to spring. In the simplicity of the house of Nazareth dwells the pure "remnant" of Israel from which God wants his people to be reborn, like a new tree that will spread its branches throughout the world, offering to all humanity the good fruit of salvation. Unlike Adam and Eve, Mary stays obedient to the Lord's will; with her whole being she speaks her "yes" and makes herself entirely available to the divine plan. She is the new Eve, the true "mother of all the living," namely, those who, because of their faith in Christ, receive eternal life.

December 12: Solemnity of the
Blessed Virgin Mary of Guadalupe

The countries of Latin America celebrated the bicentennial anniversary of their independence in 2011. Benedict XVI sought to underscore in a particular way that the path toward unity that this continent has followed has coincided with the emergence of its new role at the highest level on the global stage. It is important that these diverse peoples preserve the rich treasure of their faith, as well as their historical and cultural energy, by remaining steadfast in their defense of human life, of the family and its mission, and of those who work for peace.

The venerated image of the Madonna of Tepeyac, with her sweet and peaceful countenance, imprinted on the mantle of the Mexican Indian St. Juan Diego, shows her as "the ever Virgin Mary, Mother of the True God from whom she lives" (from the *Office of Readings: Nicán Mopohua,* 12th ed., Mexico City, D.F., 1971, 3-19). She reminds us of the "woman clothed with the sun, with the moon under her feet, and on her head a crown of twelve stars; she was with child" (Rev. 12:1-2). She signals the presence of the Savior to the indigenous and mestizo population. She always leads us to her divine Son, who is revealed as the foundation of the dignity of every human being, as a love that is stronger than the powers of evil and death, and the fountain of joy, filial trust, consolation, and hope. In this sense she, with her simplicity and maternal heart, continues to indicate the one Light and the one Truth: her Son, Jesus Christ, who is "the definitive answer to the question of the meaning of life, and to those fundamental questions which still trouble so many men and women on the American continent" (*Post-Synodal Apostolic Exhortation Ecclesia in America,* no. 10).

Third Sunday of Advent

Today in the liturgy the Apostle Paul's invitation rings out: "Rejoice in the Lord always; again I will say, rejoice. . . . The Lord is at hand!" (Phil. 4:4-5). While Mother Church accompanies us towards Holy Christmas she helps us rediscover the meaning and taste of Christian joy, so different from that of the world. It is necessary to seek to live in the reality of daily life that the crib represents, namely, the love of Christ, his humility, his poverty. This is what St. Francis did at

Greccio: he re-created a live presentation of the nativity scene in order to contemplate and worship it, but above all to be better able to put into practice the message of the Son of God who for love of us emptied himself completely and made himself a tiny child. This, dear friends, is what true joy consists in: it is feeling that our personal and community existence has been visited and filled by a great mystery, the mystery of God's love. In order to rejoice we do not need things alone, but love and truth: we need a close God who warms our hearts and responds to our deepest expectations. This God is manifested in Jesus, born of the Virgin Mary. Therefore that "Bambinello" which we place in a stable or a grotto is the center of all things, the heart of the world.

Fourth Sunday of Advent

The only moment of the liturgical year in which the pope celebrates the Eucharist wearing a rose chasuble.

With the words of the prophet Micah, the liturgy invites us to look to Bethlehem, the little town of Judea that is witness to the great event: "And you, Bethlehem-Ephrathah, too small to be among the clans of Judah, from you shall come forth for me one who is to be ruler in Israel; whose origin is from of old, from ancient times" (Mic. 5:2). One thousand years before Christ, Bethlehem had given birth to the great king David, whom the Scriptures concur in presenting as the ancestor of the Messiah. Luke's Gospel says that Jesus was born in Bethlehem because Joseph, the husband of Mary, being "of the house of David," had to return there for the census, and it was then that Mary gave birth to Jesus (cf. Luke 2:1-7). The same prophecy of Micah continues, noting a mysterious birth: "God will give them up," he says, "until the time when she who is to give birth has borne, and the rest of his brethren shall return to the children of Israel" (Mic. 5:3). There is thus a divine plan that includes and explains the times and places of the coming of the Son of God into the world. It is a plan of peace, as the prophet proclaims, saying of the Messiah: "He shall stand firm and shepherd his flock by the strength of the Lord, in the majestic name of the Lord, his God. And they shall remain, for now his greatness shall reach to the ends of the earth. He himself shall be peace!" (Mic. 5:4-5).

December 24: Christmas Eve

In St. Peter's Basilica, Benedict XVI celebrates the midnight Mass in the presence of thousands of believers who have come from all over the world. He places the Christ child in the crib in the manger that lies in St. Peter's Square, while the Sistine Chapel choir sings "Alleluia."

———

God dwells on high, yet he stoops down to us. . . . God is infinitely great, and far, far above us. This is our first experience of him. The distance seems infinite. The Creator of the universe, the one who guides all things, is very far from us: or so he seems at the beginning. But then comes the surprising realization: The One who has no equal, who "is seated on high," looks down upon us. He stoops down. He sees us, and he sees me. God's looking down is much more than simply seeing from above. God's looking is active. The fact is that he sees me, that he looks at me, transforms me and the world around me. The Psalm [113 (112)] tells us this in the following verse: "He raises the poor from the dust. . . ." In looking down, he raises me up; he takes me gently by the hand and helps me — me! — to rise from the depths towards the heights. "God stoops down." This is a prophetic word. That night in Bethlehem, it took on a completely new meaning. God's stooping down became real in a way previously inconceivable. He stoops down — he himself comes down as a child to the lowly stable, the symbol of all humanity's neediness and forsakenness. God truly comes down. He becomes a child and puts himself in the state of complete dependence typical of a newborn child.

The Christmas Season

December 25: Christmas

Benedict XVI continues the tradition of papal Christmas hom-
ilies and pronounces his Urbi et Orbi *message to the city and*
to the world from the Loggia at St. Peter's. He delivers his good
wishes to the believers in fifty-six languages.

"Apparuit gratia Dei Salvatoris nostri omnibus hominibus"
(Titus 2:11). The meaning of Christmas, and more generally the
meaning of the liturgical year, is precisely to bring us closer to
these divine signs to see their imprint in day-to-day events.

The cycle of the Christmas solemnities leads us to meditate
on the birth of Jesus, announced by the angels who were sur-

rounded with the luminous splendor of God; the Christmas season speaks to us of the star that guided the Magi of the East to the house in Bethlehem, and invites us to look to heaven, which opens above the Jordan as God's voice resounds. These are all signs through which the Lord never tires of repeating: "Yes, I am here. I know you. I love you. There is a path that leads from me to you. And there is a path that rises from you to me." The Creator assumed the dimensions of a child in Jesus, of a human being like us, to make himself visible and tangible. At the same time, by making himself small, God caused the light of his greatness to shine. For precisely by lowering himself to the point of defenseless vulnerability of love, he shows what his true greatness is indeed, what it means to be God. That is why Christmas is a feast of light. Not like the full daylight that illumines everything, but a glimmer beginning in the night and spreading out from a precise point in the universe: from the stable of Bethlehem, where the divine Child was born. Indeed, he is the light itself, which begins to radiate, as portrayed in so many paintings of the Nativity. He is the light whose appearance breaks through the gloom, dispels the darkness, and enables us to understand the meaning and the value of our own lives and of all history. Jesus — the face of the "God who saves" — did not show himself only for a certain few, but for everyone. Although it is true that in the simple and lowly dwelling of Bethlehem few persons encountered him, still he came for all: Jews and Gentiles, rich and poor, those near and those far away, believers and nonbelievers . . . for everyone.

December 26: St. Stephen Martyr

In St. Stephen we see the realization of the first fruits of salvation that Christ's birth brought to the human race: the victory of life over death, of love over hatred, of the light of truth over the darkness of falsehood.

Stephen, a young man "full of faith and of the Holy Spirit," as he is described in the Acts of the Apostles (6:5), together with another six men, was ordained a deacon in the first community of Jerusalem and, because of his passionate and courageous preaching, was arrested and stoned. There is one detail in the account of his martyrdom that should be emphasized, and it is the remark: "the witnesses laid down their garments at the feet of a young man named Saul" (Acts

7:58). Here, with his Hebrew name of Saul, St. Paul appears for the first time in the guise of a zealous persecutor of the Church (cf. Phil. 3:6), which he then perceived as a duty and as something to boast of. It could be said *a posteriori* that precisely Stephen's witness was decisive for his conversion. Shortly after Stephen's martyrdom, Saul, still driven by zeal against the Christians, went to Damascus to arrest those he would find there. And while he was approaching the city the blinding flash occurred, that unique experience in which the risen Jesus appeared to him, spoke to him, and changed his life (cf. Acts 9:1-9). When Saul, having fallen to the ground, heard himself called by name by a mysterious voice and asked: "Who are you, O Lord?," he heard the answer: "I am Jesus, whom you are persecuting" (Acts 9:5).

The Feast of the Holy Family

Mary and Joseph cooperated with the Lord's plan of salvation, and Christmas is the feast of the family par excellence. This is shown by the different traditions and social customs that exist, in particular the practice of getting together, especially as a family, to share a Christmas meal and to exchange good wishes and presents. But we also have to recognize that in these circumstances we experience even more acutely the difficulties and sufferings that are produced by the wounds of familial life.

———

Jesus willed to be born and to grow up in a human family; he had the Virgin Mary as his mother and Joseph who acted as his father; they raised and educated him with immense love. Jesus' family truly deserves the title "Holy," for it was fully engaged in the desire to do the will of God, incarnate in the adorable presence of Jesus. On the one hand, it was a family like all others and as such, it is a model of conjugal love, collaboration, sacrifice, and entrustment to divine Providence, hard work, and solidarity — in short, of all those values that the family safeguards and promotes, making an important contribution to forming the fabric of every society. At the same time, however, the Family of Nazareth was unique, different from all other families because of its singular vocation linked to the mission of the Son of God. With precisely this uniqueness it points out to every family and in the first place to Christian families God's horizon, the sweet and demanding primacy of his will, the prospect of heaven to which we are all destined.

December 31:
Recitation of the *Te Deum* in Thanksgiving

According to the tradition, the pope brings the year to a close in the Jesuit Church of the Gesu in Rome.

———

"*O admirabile commercium!* O marvelous exchange!" Thus begins the antiphon of the first Psalm, to then continue: "man's Creator has become man, born of a virgin." Thus everything this evening invites us to turn our gaze to the one who "received the Word of God in her heart and in her body and gave Life to the world," and for this very reason, as the Second Vatican Ecumenical Council recalls, "is acknowledged and honored as being truly the Mother of God" (*Lumen Gentium,* n. 53). Christ's Nativity, which we are commemorating in these days, is entirely suffused with the light of Mary and, while we pause at the manger to contemplate the Child, our gaze cannot fail to turn in gratitude also to his Mother, who with her "yes" made possible the gift of redemption. This is why the Christmas season brings with it a profoundly Marian connotation; the birth of Jesus as God and man and Mary's divine motherhood are inseparable realities; the mystery of Mary and the mystery of the only-begotten Son of God who was made man form a single mystery, in which the one helps to better understand the other.

January 1: Solemnity of Mary, the Mother of God

The first of January is also the world day of peace, as decreed by Pope Paul VI. Every year on this date the pope delivers a message of peace to all people of goodwill.

Thus the ancient Jewish tradition of blessing is brought to completion (Num. 6:22-27): the priests of Israel blessed the people by putting the Lord's Name upon them: "so shall they put my name upon the people of Israel." With a triple formula present in the first reading, the sacred Name was invoked upon the faithful three times, as a wish for grace and peace. This remote custom brings us back to an essential reality: to be able to walk in the way of peace, men and women and peoples need to be illumined by the "Face" of God and to be blessed by his "Name." Precisely this came about definitively with the incarnation: the coming of the Son of God in our flesh and in history brought an irrevocable blessing, a light that is never to be extinguished, and offers believers and people of good will alike the possibility of building the civilization of love and peace. The earthly history of Jesus that culminated in the Paschal Mystery is the beginning of a new world, because he truly inaugurated a new humanity, ever and only with Christ's grace, capable of bringing about a peaceful "revolution." This revolution was not an ideological but a spiritual revolution, not utopian but real, and for this reason in need of infinite patience, sometimes of very long periods, avoiding any shortcuts and taking the hardest path: the path of the development of responsibility in consciences.

January 6: Epiphany of the Lord

This is the feast day that brings the Christmas season to a close. It is one of the most respected religious feast days in Italy.

Epiphany, the "manifestation" of Our Lord Jesus Christ, is a many-faceted mystery. The Latin tradition identifies it with the visit of the Magi to the infant Jesus in Bethlehem and thus interprets it above all as a revelation of the Messiah of Israel to the Gentiles. The Eastern tradition on the other hand gives priority to the moment of Jesus' Baptism in the River Jordan when he manifested himself as the only-begotten Son of the heavenly Father, consecrated by the Holy Spirit. John's Gospel, however, also invites us to consider as an "epiphany" the wedding at Cana, during which, by changing the water into wine, Jesus "manifested his glory; and his disciples believed in him" (John 2:11). And what should we say, dear brothers and sisters, especially we priests of the New Covenant who are everyday witnesses and ministers of the "epiphany" of Jesus Christ in the Holy Eucharist? The Church celebrates all the mysteries of the Lord in this most holy and most humble sacrament in which he both reveals and conceals his glory.

January 13: Baptism of the Lord

Every year, the pope celebrates a Mass in the Sistine Chapel during which he confers the sacrament of baptism on newborn children.

With the feast of the Lord's Baptism, which concludes the

Octave of the Epiphany, the Christmas season comes to an end. According to the Christian tradition, children are baptized by being introduced into the light of God and of his teachings; they are given the wealth of the divine life in which true freedom has its roots, the freedom that belongs to the children of God. This is a freedom that will need to be educated and formed over the course of many years in order that the children may become capable of responsible personal choices.

And if Christmas and Epiphany serve above all to make us capable of seeing, to opening our eyes and hearts to the mystery of a God who comes to be with us, the feast of the Baptism of Jesus introduces us, we could say, to the everydayness of a personal relationship with him. In fact, through the immersion in the waters of the Jordan, Jesus united himself to us. Baptism is, so to speak, the bridge that he has built between him and us, the road by which he is accessible to us; it is the divine rainbow over our life, the promise of the great yes of God, the gateway to hope and, at the same time, the sign that indicates the road we must take in an active and joyous way to meet him and feel loved by him. From the time that the only-begotten Son of the Father was baptized, heaven has truly opened and continues to open itself, and we can entrust every new life that blossoms to the hands of God, who is stronger than the dark powers of evil. This in effect leads to baptism: We restore to God that which has come from him. The child is not the parents' property, but is rather entrusted by the Creator to their responsibility, freely and in an ever-new way, so that they help him to be a free child of God.

Ordinary Time: After Epiphany

January 25: The Conversion of St. Paul

On this feast day of unity par excellence, the pope gathers around himself a number of religious personages from different Christian faith traditions, whether they be Orthodox or Protestant, for a ceremony that has traditionally taken place in St. Paul Outside the Walls.

The "Conversion of St. Paul" shows us the true meaning of conversion in the gospel — metanoia — if we consider the apostle's experience. To be sure, there are some who prefer to avoid applying this term to St. Paul, because they say that he was already a believer, and indeed even a fervent Jew, and that is why he did not pass from nonbelief to faith, from idols to God, and did not have to abandon the Jewish faith in order to follow Christ. But in reality, the experience of the apostle can be the model of every authentic Christian conversion. St. Paul's experience provides the paradigm of conversion and shows us the path we must follow to find full unity.

———

Converting means, for each one of us also, believing that Jesus "gave himself up for me," dying on the cross (cf. Gal. 2:20) and, risen, lives with me and in me. Entrusting myself to the power of his forgiveness, letting myself be led by the hand by him, I can get out of the quicksand of pride and sin, of lies and sadness, of selfishness and every false certainty, to know and live the richness of his love. This new road cannot come from us. It consists in letting ourselves be conquered by Christ. This is why St. Paul does not say: "I converted" but rather "I died" (Gal. 2:19), I am a new creature. In reality, St. Paul's conversion was not a passage from immorality to morality, from a mistaken faith to a right faith, but it was a being conquered by Christ: the renunciation of his own perfection; it was the humility of one who puts himself without reserve in the service of Christ for the brethren. And only in this renunciation of ourselves, in this conforming to Christ, are we also united among ourselves; we become "one" in

Christ. It is communion with the risen Christ that gives us unity.

February 2:
The Presentation of the Lord at the Temple
(Candlemass)

A feast day for consecrated men and women. The pope addresses them from a balcony inside St. Peter's Basilica, which opens onto the Loggia of the Blessings.

What is the consecrated life if not a radical imitation of Jesus, a total "sequela" of his person? (cf. Matt. 19:27-28). Following Jesus represents a privileged way to respond, faithfully to the end, to a special vocation of consecration and mission in the Church.

From his own voice we can recognize a lifestyle that expresses the substance of consecrated life inspired by the evangelical counsels of poverty, chastity, and obedience. He sees the life of *poverty* as the guarantee of a gospel proclamation carried out totally gratuitously (cf. 1 Cor. 9:1-23) while at the same time he expresses concrete solidarity to his brethren in need. In this regard we all know of Paul's decision to support himself with the work of his hands and of his commitment to collecting offerings for the poor of Jerusalem (cf. 1 Thess. 2:9; 2 Cor. 8–9). Paul is also an apostle who, in accepting God's call to *chastity,* gave his heart to the Lord in an undivided manner to be able to serve his brethren with even greater freedom and dedication (cf. 1 Cor. 7:7; 2 Cor. 11:1-2). Furthermore, in a world in which the values of Christian chastity were far from widespread (cf. 1 Cor. 6:12-20) he offered a reliable reference for conduct. Then concerning *obedience,* it suffices to note that doing God's will and the "daily pressure upon me of my anxiety for all the churches" (2 Cor. 11:28) motivated, shaped, and consummated his existence, rendered a sacrifice that found favor with God. All this brought him to proclaim, as he wrote to the Philippians: "For to me to live is Christ, and to die is gain" (Phil. 1:21).

February 11:
The Solemnity of the Blessed Virgin of Lourdes

John Paul II established this feast day for the sick. The Virgin of Lourdes is exposed upon the altar at which the pope celebrates the Mass.

This feast invites us to help the sick to experience in a much more intense way the spiritual intimacy of the Church, who, as the pope said in the encyclical Deus Caritas Est, *is God's family in the world. Inside this family, no one ought to suffer the lack of any necessity, and above all the lack of love.*

———————

The significance of suffering, sickness, and death remains unfathomable to our minds. However, the light of faith comes to our aid. The Word of God reveals to us that these evils are also mysteriously "embraced" by the design of salvation. Faith helps us to uphold the belief that human life is beautiful and worthy to be lived to the full, even when undermined by sickness. God created man for happiness and for life, while sickness and death came into the world as a consequence of sin. But the Lord has not left us to ourselves. He, the Father of life, is doctor par excellence to man and never ceases his loving attentions to humanity. The gospel shows Jesus who "casts out spirits by his word and heals all of the sick" (Matt. 8:16), indicating the path of conversion and faith as conditions for obtaining the healing of the body and the soul, which is the healing that the Lord always sought. It is an integral healing, of body and soul, and that is why he casts out spirits by his word. His word is the word of love, a purifying word: it casts out the spirits of fear, of solitude, of opposition to God, in order thus to purify our soul and give it interior peace. Thus, he gives us the spirit of love and the healing that is born from within. But Jesus did not only speak; he is the Word incarnate. He suffered with us, and he died. With his passion and death, he has assumed and transformed our weakness to the very end.

Lent

At the beginning of Lent, which represents an intense path of spiritual training, the liturgy proposes three penitential practices that are precious to the biblical and Christian tradition — prayer, almsgiving, and fasting — in order to prepare oneself to celebrate Easter more properly and thus to have the experience of the power of God who "triumphs over evil, washes away our sins, restores innocence to sinners, joy to the afflicted, extinguishes hatred, brings us peace and humbles the proud in the world" (Easter Proclamation). Lent recalls to us the forty days of fasting that the Lord underwent in the desert, prior to commencing his public mission. The Holy Scriptures and the entire Christian tradi-

tion teach that fasting is a great help to avoid sin and everything that leads to it. That is why, in the history of salvation, the invitation to fast recurs time after time. The faithful practice of fasting contributes to the unification of the human person, body and soul, by helping one to avoid sin and to grow in intimacy with the Lord.

Ash Wednesday

According to the pontifical tradition, the Mass for Ash Wednesday is celebrated in the Basilica of St. Anselm on the Aventine.

This day is considered the liturgical gateway into Lent.

The appeal for conversion emerges as a dominant theme in every component of today's liturgy. Already in the entrance antiphon, it states that the Lord overlooks and forgives the sins of those who repent; in the Collect, Christian people are invited to pray so that each one may undertake a "journey of true conversion." In the First Reading, the prophet Joel urges us to return to the Father "with your whole heart, with fasting, with weeping, and with mourning. . . . For he is gracious and merciful, slow to anger, rich in kindness, and relenting in punishment" (2:12-13). God's promise is clear: if the people will listen to the invitation to conversion, God will make his mercy triumph and his friends will be showered with countless favors. With the Responsorial Psalm, the liturgical assembly makes the invocations of Psalm 51[50] its own, asking the Lord to create within us "a clean heart" and to renew in us "a right spirit." Next is the Gospel passage in which Jesus warns us against the canker of vanity that leads to ostentation and hypocrisy, to superficiality and self-satisfaction, and reasserts the need to foster uprightness of heart. At the same time he shows us the means to grow in this purity of intention: by cultivating intimacy with the heavenly Father.

First Sunday of Lent

The Gospel, in the sober and concise style of St. Mark, introduces us into the atmosphere of this liturgical season:

"The Spirit drove Jesus out into the desert, and he remained in the desert for forty days, tempted by Satan" (Mark 1:12). In the succinct account, angels, luminous and mysterious figures, appear almost fleetingly before this dark, tenebrous figure who dares to tempt the Lord. Angels, the Gospel says, "ministered" to Jesus (Mark 1:13); they are the antithesis of Satan. "Angel" means "messenger." Throughout the Old Testament we find these figures who help and guide human beings on God's behalf. It suffices to remember the Book of Tobit, in which the figure of the angel Raphael appears and assists the protagonist in every vicissitude. The reassuring presence of the angel of the Lord accompanies the people of Israel in all of their experiences, good and bad. On the threshold of the New Testament, Gabriel is dispatched to announce to Zechariah and to Mary the joyful events at the beginning of our salvation; and an angel (we are not told his name) warns Joseph, guiding him in that moment of uncertainty. A choir of angels brings the shepherds the good news of the Savior's birth; and it was also to be angels who announced the joyful news of his resurrection to the women. At the end of time, angels will accompany Jesus when he comes in his glory (cf. Matt. 25:31).

Second Sunday of Lent

This has been a week of silence and prayer: our minds and hearts could be entirely focused on God, listening to his word, meditating on the mysteries of Christ. To summarize, it is a bit like what happened to the Apostles Peter, James, and John when Jesus took them with him up a high mountain, and while he prayed he was "transfigured": his face and his garments became luminous, glistening (cf. Mark 9:2-10). Jesus wanted his disciples, in particular those who would be responsible for guiding the nascent Church, to have a direct experience of his divine glory, so that they could face the scandal of the Cross. Indeed, when the hour of betrayal came and Jesus withdrew to the Garden of Gethsemane, he kept the same disciples — Peter, James, and John — close to him, asking them to watch and pray with him (cf. Matt. 26:38). They were not to succeed in doing so, but the grace of Christ was to sustain them and help them to believe in the resurrection. The Transfiguration of Jesus was essentially an experience of prayer (cf. Luke 9:28-29). Indeed, prayer reaches its culmination and thus becomes a source of inner light when the spirit of the human being adheres to that of God, and their respective wills merge, as it were, to become a whole. When Jesus went up the mountain, he was immersed in contemplation of the loving plan of the Father, who had sent him into the world to save humanity. Elijah and Moses appeared beside Jesus, meaning that the sacred Scriptures were in concordance with the proclamation of his Paschal Mystery.

February 22: The Feast of the Chair of Peter

The feast of the Chair of Peter is an important liturgical celebration that sheds light on the ministry of the Successor of the Prince of the Apostles. This celebration is the occasion for the pope to ask the faithful to accompany him in their prayers, so that he might faithfully carry out the noble task that divine Providence has entrusted to him as the Successor to the Apostle Peter.

The Chair of Peter symbolizes the authority of the Bishop of Rome, called to carry out a special service to the entire people of God. Immediately after the martyrdom of Saints Peter and Paul, the primatial role of the Church of Rome in the whole Catholic community was recognized. This role was already attested to at the beginning of the second century by St. Ignatius of Antioch (*Epistula ad Romanos,* Pref., ed. Funk, i, p. 252) and by St. Irenaeus of Lyons (*Adversus haereses* III, 3, 2-3). This singular and specific ministry of the Bishop of Rome was reaffirmed by the Second Vatican Council. "In the communion of the Church," we read in the Dogmatic Constitution on the Church, "there are also particular Churches that retain their own traditions, without prejudice to the Chair of Peter which presides over the whole assembly of charity (cf. St. Ignatius of Antioch, *Ep. ad Rom.,* Pref.), and protects their legitimate variety while at the same time taking care that these differences do not hinder unity, but rather contribute to it" (*Lumen Gentium,* n. 13).

Annunciation

A wonderful mystery of the faith that we contemplate every day as we recite the Angelus.

The Annunciation, recounted at the beginning of St. Luke's Gospel, is a humble, hidden event — no one saw it, no one except Mary knew of it — , but at the same time it was crucial to the history of humanity. When the Virgin said her "yes" to the angel's announcement, Jesus was conceived and with him began the new era of history that was to be ratified in Easter as the "new and eternal covenant." In fact, Mary's "yes" perfectly mirrors that of Christ himself when he entered the world, as the Letter to the Hebrews says, interpreting Psalm 40[39]: "As is written of me in the book, I have come to do your will, O God" (Heb. 10:7). The Son's obedience was reflected in that of the Mother and thus, through the encounter of these two "yeses," God was able to take on a human face. This is why the Annunciation is a Christological feast as well, because it celebrates a central mystery of Christ: the incarnation.

Third Sunday of Lent

The liturgy again presents one of the most beautiful and profound passages of the Bible: the dialogue between Jesus and the Samaritan woman (cf. John 4:5-42). St. Augustine, of whom I am speaking extensively in the Wednesday Catecheses, was justifiably fascinated by this narrative, and he made a memorable comment on it. It is impossible to give a brief explanation of the wealth of this Gospel passage. One must read and meditate on it personally, identifying oneself with that woman who, one day like so many other days, went to draw water from the well and found Jesus there, sitting next to it, "tired from the journey" in the midday heat. "Give me a drink," he said, leaving her very surprised: it was in fact completely out of the ordinary that a Jew would speak to a Samaritan woman, and all the more so to a stranger. But the woman's bewilderment was destined to increase. Jesus spoke of a "living water" able to quench her thirst and become in her "a spring of water welling up to eternal life"; in addition, he demonstrated that he knew her personal life; he revealed that the hour has come to adore the one true God in spirit and truth; and lastly, he entrusted her with something extremely rare: that he is the Messiah. All this began from the real and notable experience of thirst. The theme of thirst runs throughout John's Gospel: from the meeting with the Samaritan woman to the great prophecy during the feast of Tabernacles (John 7:37-38), even to the Cross, when Jesus, before he dies, said in order to fulfill the Scriptures: "I thirst" (John 19:28). Christ's thirst is an entranceway to the mystery of God, who became thirsty to satisfy our thirst, just as he became poor to make us rich (cf. 2 Cor. 8:9). Yes, God thirsts for our faith and our love.

Fourth Sunday of Lent

The liturgy takes us on a true and proper baptismal route through the texts of John's Gospel: by healing the man born blind, he reveals himself as "the light of the world" (John 9:1-41). According to the common mentality of the time, the disciples take it for granted that the man's blindness was the result of a sin committed by him or his parents. Jesus, however, rejects this prejudice and says: "It was not that this man sinned, or his parents, but that the works of God might be made manifest in him" (John 9:3). What comfort these words offer us! They let us hear the living voice of God, who is provident and wise Love! In the face of men and women marked by limitations and suffering, Jesus did not think of their possible guilt but rather of the will of God who created man for life. And so he solemnly declares: "We must work the works of him who sent me. . . . As long as I am in the world, I am the light of the world" (John 9:4-5). And he immediately takes action: mixing a little earth with saliva, he made mud and spread it on the eyes of the blind man. This act alludes to the creation of man, which the Bible recounts using the symbol of dust from the ground, fashioned and enlivened by God's breath (Gen. 2:7). In fact, "Adam" means "ground" and the human body was in effect formed of particles of soil. By healing the blind man Jesus worked a new creation. But this healing sparked heated debate because Jesus did it on the Sabbath, thereby in the Pharisees' opinion violating the feast-day precept. Thus, at the end of the account, Jesus and the blind man are both cast out, the former because he broke the law and the latter because, despite being healed, he remained marked as a sinner from birth. Jesus reveals to the blind man whom he had healed that he had come into the world for judgment, to separate the blind who can be healed from those who do not allow themselves to be healed because they consider themselves healthy.

March 19: The Solemnity of St. Joseph

This feast day is all the more important because St. Joseph is Benedict XVI's heavenly Patron. Benedict XVI also celebrates his own feast day on this date, because his name is Joseph. The liturgy does not forget the teacher of Christ.

Joseph is the man who has given to God the greatest proof of his trust in all of history.

———

We are asking the Lord to protect the Church always — and he does! — just as Joseph protected his family and kept watch over the child Jesus during his early years. Our Gospel reading recalls this for us. The angel said to Joseph: "Do not be afraid to take Mary your wife into your home" (Matt. 1:20), and that is precisely what he did: "he did as the angel of the Lord had commanded him" (Matt. 1:24). Why was St. Matthew so keen to note Joseph's trust in the words received from the messenger of God, if not to invite us to imitate this same loving trust? [With respect to Joseph,] the prophet Nathan, in obedience to God's command, tells David: "I will raise up your heir after you, sprung from your loins" (2 Sam. 7:12). David must accept that he will die before seeing the fulfillment of this promise, which will come to pass "when (his) time comes" and he will rest "with (his) ancestors." We thus come to realize that one of humankind's most cherished desires — seeing the fruits of one's labors — is not always granted by God. What God asks David to do is to place his trust in him. David himself will not see his heir who will have a throne "firm forever" (2 Sam. 7:16), for this heir, announced under the veil of prophecy, is Jesus. David puts his trust in God. In the same way, Joseph trusts God when he hears his messenger, the angel, say to him: "Joseph, son of David, do not be afraid to take Mary your wife into your home. For it is through the Holy Spirit that this child has been conceived in her" (Matt. 1:20).

Fifth Sunday of Lent

In our Lenten journey we have reached the Fifth Sunday, characterized by the Gospel of the resurrection of Lazarus (John 11:1-45). It concerns the last "sign" fulfilled by Jesus, after which the chief priests convened the Sanhedrin and deliberated killing him, and decided to kill the same Lazarus who was living proof of the divinity of Christ, the Lord of life and death. Actually, this Gospel passage shows Jesus as true Man and true God. First of all, the Evangelist insists on his friendship with Lazarus and his sisters, Martha and Mary. He emphasizes that "Jesus loved" them (John 11:5), and this is why he wanted to accomplish the great wonder. "Our friend Lazarus has fallen asleep, but I go to awaken him out of sleep" (John 11:11), he tells his disciples, expressing God's viewpoint on physical death with the metaphor of sleep. God sees it exactly as sleep, from which he can awaken us. Jesus has shown an absolute power regarding this death, seen when he gives life back to the widow of Nain's young son (cf. Luke 7:11-17) and to the twelve-year-old girl (cf. Mark 5:35-43). Precisely concerning her he said: "The child is not dead but sleeping" (Mark 5:39), attracting the derision of those present. But in truth it is exactly like this: bodily death is a sleep from which God can awaken us at any moment.

Palm Sunday

In 1982, John Paul II inaugurated the World Youth Days, which take place each year at the diocesan level on Palm Sunday.

Have we really understood the message of Jesus, the Son of David? Have we understood the nature of the Kingdom that he spoke about during his interrogation before Pilate? Do we understand what it means to say that this Kingdom is not of this world? Or would we instead prefer that it be of this world?

In St. John's Gospel, after the account of the entry into Jerusalem, there follows a series of sayings in which Jesus explains the essential content of this new kind of Kingdom. On a first reading of these texts, we can distinguish three different images of the Kingdom in which the same mystery is reflected in a number of different ways. John recounts, first of all, that during the feast there were some Greeks among the pilgrims who "wanted to adore God" (cf. 12:20). Let us note the fact that the true intention of these pilgrims was to adore God. This corresponds perfectly to what Jesus says on the occasion of the cleansing of the Temple: "My house shall be called a house of prayer for all the nations" (Mark 11:17). The true purpose of the pilgrimage must be that of encountering God; adoring him, and thus rightly ordering the fundamental relationship of our life. The Greeks are searching for God; their lives are a journey towards God. Now, through the two Greek-speaking apostles, Philip and Andrew, they convey this request to the Lord: "We wish to see Jesus" (John 12:21). These are stirring words: we wish to see Jesus.

The Paschal Triduum

During the Paschal Triduum, the liturgy invites us to meditate on the passion, death, and resurrection of the Lord. The rites of the chrismal Mass express the fullness of Christ's priesthood as well as the ecclesial communion that ought to animate the Christian people gathered for the eucharistic sacrifice and brought to life in unity by the gift of the Holy Spirit. During the evening Mass, the Church commemorates the institution of the Eucharist, the ministerial priesthood, and the new commandment of love that Jesus left to his disciples. This celebration invites us to give thanks to God for the gift of the Eucharist. Commemorating the passion and death of Jesus on the Cross, Good Friday is a day of sadness, but at the same time it is the propitious moment for awakening our faith, for strengthening our hope and our courage so that we might bear our cross with humility and trust in God, sure of his support and his victory. In the great silence of Holy Saturday, the Church keeps vigil in prayer, sharing Mary's experiences of suffering and trust in God. This moment of recollection will lead to the Paschal vigil, in which the joy of Easter will burst forth. Thus, the victory of light over darkness will be proclaimed, the victory of life over death, and the Church will rejoice in her encounter with her Lord.

Holy Thursday

Chrism Mass

The pope celebrates Mass in the morning in St. Peter's Basilica.

The Lord requires the sanctification, the consecration of the priests in the truth. And he sends them out, each of them, to follow his own mission.

We need first to clarify what the Bible means by the words "holy" and "sanctify — consecrate." "Holy" — this word describes above all God's own nature, his completely unique, divine way of being, one which is his alone. He alone is the true and authentic Holy One, in the original sense of the word. All other holiness derives from him, is a participation in his way of being. He is purest Light, Truth, and untainted Good. To consecrate something or someone means, therefore, to give that thing or person to God as his property, to take it out of the context of what is ours and to insert it in God's milieu, so that it no longer belongs to our affairs, but is totally of God. Consecration is thus a taking away from the world and a giving over to the living God. The thing or person no longer belongs to us, or even to itself, but is immersed in God. Such a giving up of something in order to give it over to God, we also call a sacrifice: this thing will no longer be my property, but his property.

The Paschal Triduum

Mass of the Lord's Supper

The pope celebrates Mass at the end of the afternoon in the cathedral of Rome in which the bishop's chair resides, the Church of St. John Lateran.

The Church commemorates the institution of the Eucharist, the ministerial priesthood, and the new commandment of love that Jesus gave to his disciples.

———

St. Paul offers one of the oldest accounts of what happened in the Upper Room, on the vigil of the Lord's Passion. "The Lord Jesus," he writes at the beginning of the 50s, on the basis of a text he received from the Lord's own environment, "on the night in which he was betrayed took bread, and after he had given thanks, broke it and said, 'This is my body, which is for you. Do this in remembrance of me.' In the same way, after the supper, he took the cup, saying, 'This cup is the new covenant in my blood. Do this, whenever you drink it, in remembrance of me'" (1 Cor. 11:23-25). These words, laden with mystery, clearly show Christ's will: under the species of the Bread and the Wine, he makes himself present with his body given and his blood poured out. This is the sacrifice of the new and everlasting covenant offered to all, without distinction of race or culture. It is from this sacramental rite, which he presents to the Church as the supreme evidence of his love, that Jesus makes ministers of his disciples and all those who will continue the ministry through the centuries. Thus, Holy Thursday constitutes a renewed invitation to give thanks to God for the supreme gift of the Eucharist, to receive with devotion and to adore with living faith.

Good Friday

Good Friday is the day of the Lord's Passion and Crucifixion. In the afternoon, the pope offers the sacrament of confession in St. Peter's Basilica. That night, he leads the Via Crucis in the Coliseum.

———————

Jesus wanted to offer his life in sacrifice for the remission of humanity's sins. As it does before the Eucharist, as well as before the Passion and death of Jesus on the Cross, the mystery eludes reason. We are placed before something which, humanly, may appear senseless: a God who is not only made

Man, with all the needs of man, who not only suffers to save man, taking upon himself the whole tragedy of humanity, but also dies for man. Christ's death recalls the accumulated sorrow and evils that weigh upon humanity of every age: the crushing weight of our death, the hatred and violence that still today stain the earth with blood. The Passion of the Lord continues in the suffering of human beings. As Blaise Pascal has rightly written: "Jesus will be in agony even to the end of the world. We must not sleep during that time" (*Pensées,* 553). If Good Friday is a day full of sorrow, it is therefore at the same time a particularly propitious day to reawaken our faith, to consolidate our hope and courage so that each one of us may carry our cross with humility, trust, and abandonment in God, certain of his support and his victory. The liturgy of this day sings: *O Crux, ave, spes unica* — Hail, O Cross, our only hope!

Holy Saturday

The Paschal vigil takes place in St. Peter's Basilica. The pope confers the sacrament of baptism on catechumens from the five continents of the world.

Holy Saturday

This is the time of hope. This hope nourishes itself in the great silence of Holy Saturday, in the expectant waiting for the Lord's resurrection. On this day, the churches are stripped bare and no particular liturgical rite is meant to be performed. The Church keeps prayerful vigil like Mary and with Mary, by sharing the same experiences of suffering and of trust in God. It is rightly recommended that people spend the entire day in a spirit of prayer, which disposes one to meditation and reconciliation; believers are encouraged to avail themselves of the sacrament of penance in order that they might be genuinely renewed in their participation in the celebration of Easter. During the night, the recollection and the silence of Holy Saturday lead into the solemn Easter Vigil, the "mother of all vigils," when the song of joy over the resurrection of Christ resounds in all the churches and communities. The victory of light over darkness, of life over death, is proclaimed once more, and the Church will rejoice in meeting her Lord. This is how we enter into the spirit of Easter and the resurrection.

Easter

The pope delivers the Urbi et Orbi *message from the Loggia of St. Peter's Basilica and gives his blessing.*

———

One of the questions that most preoccupies men and women is this: What is there after death? To this mystery today's solemnity allows us to respond that death does not have the last word, because Life will be victorious at the end. This certainty of ours is based not on simple human reasoning, but on a historical fact of faith: Jesus Christ, crucified and buried, is risen with his glorified body. Jesus is risen so that we too, believing in him, may have eternal life. The resurrection, then, is not a theory, but a historical reality revealed by the man Jesus Christ by means of his "Passover," his "passage," which has opened a "new way" between heaven and earth (cf. Heb. 10:20). It is neither a myth nor a dream, it is not a vision or a utopia, it is not a fairy tale, but it is a singular and unrepeatable event: Jesus of Nazareth, son of Mary, who at dusk on Friday was taken down from the Cross and buried, has victoriously left the tomb. *Resurrectio Domini, spes nostra!* The resurrection of Christ is our hope! This the Church proclaims today with joy. She announces the hope that is now firm and invincible because God has raised Jesus Christ from the dead. She communicates the hope that she carries in her heart and wishes to share with all people in every place.

The Easter Season

Easter Monday

In the Paschal Mystery the words of Scripture are fulfilled, that is, this death that happened "according to the Scriptures" is an event that carries in itself a logos, a logic; the death of Christ testifies that the Word of God had become "flesh" to the very depth, it had become part of human "history." How and why this took place one understands from the other addition that St. Paul makes: Christ died "for our sins." With these words, the Pauline text takes up the prophecy of Isaiah contained in the Fourth Song of the Servant of God (cf. Isa. 53:12). The Servant of God, says the song, "stripped himself to death"; he carried "the sins of many," and interceding for the "sinful," was able to bring the gift of reconciliation to men among themselves and of men with God: his death therefore put an end to death itself; the way of the Cross leads to the resurrection. Not a few exegetes have seen in this expression, "He rose again on the third day, according to the Scriptures," a significant recall of what we read in Psalm 16, where the Psalmist proclaims: "For you will not abandon me to Sheol [the underworld], nor let your faithful servant see the pit" (v. 10). This is one of the Old Testament texts, often cited in early Christianity, to prove the messianic character of Jesus. Since according to Judaic interpretation, corruption [of the body] begins after the third day, the word of Scripture is fulfilled in Jesus who rises on the third day, before corruption can set in. St. Paul, faithfully transmitting the teaching of the apostles, underscores that the victory of Christ over death takes place through the creative power of God. This divine power brings hope and joy: this is the definitive liberating content of the Paschal revelation.

Divine Mercy Sunday (in Albis)

John Paul II introduced Divine Mercy Sunday.

Indeed, the Gospel recounts that at the moment of the Passion, when the divine Teacher was arrested and condemned to death, the disciples dispersed. Only Mary and the women, with the Apostle John, stayed together and followed him to Calvary. Risen, Jesus gave his disciples a new unity, stronger than before, invincible because it was founded not on human resources but on divine mercy, which made them all feel loved and forgiven by him. It is therefore God's merciful love that firmly unites the Church, today as in the past, and makes humanity a single family; divine love which through the crucified and risen Jesus forgives us our sins and renews us from within. Just as it was for the first community, it is Mary who accompanies us in our everyday life. We call upon her as "Queen of Heaven," knowing that her regal character is like that of her Son: all love and merciful love.

Third Sunday of Easter

In today's Gospel, St. Luke recounts one of the apparitions of the risen Christ (24:35-48). At the start of this passage, the evangelist notes that the two disciples of Emmaus, who returned in haste to Jerusalem, related to the Eleven how they recognized the Lord "in the breaking of bread" (v. 35). And while they were recalling this extraordinary experience of their encounter with the Lord, "he stood in their midst" (v. 36). Because of his unexpected apparition, the apostles were startled and terrified, to the point that Jesus, to reassure them and overcome their every hesitation and doubt, asked them to touch him — he was not a phantasm, but a man of flesh and bone — and then, he asked them for something to eat. Once more, as it had been with the two disciples at Emmaus, it is at table, eating with his own people, that the risen Christ manifests himself to the disciples, helping them to understand the Scriptures and to reread the events of salvation in the light of Easter. "Everything written about me," he said to them, "in the law of Moses and the Prophets and the Psalms must be fulfilled" (v. 44). And he invited them to look to the future: "repentance and forgiveness of sins [shall] be preached in his name to all the nations" (v. 47).

Fourth Sunday of Easter, or Good Shepherd Sunday

Following a beautiful tradition, on the Sunday of the "Good Shepherd," the Bishop of Rome reunites with his presbyterium for the ordination of new diocesan priests. To become a priest in the Church means to enter into Christ's gift of self through the sacrament of holy orders, and indeed to enter into it with the whole of one's self.

"This [Jesus] is the stone . . . there is no other name . . . given among men by which we must be saved" (Acts 4:11-12). In the passage of the Acts of the Apostles (the First Reading) the singular "homonymy" between Peter and Jesus strikes us and makes us reflect: Peter, who received his name from Jesus himself, here asserts that he, Jesus, is "the stone." In fact, the only true rock is Jesus. The only name that saves is his. The apostle, and therefore the priest, receives his "name," his very identity, from Christ. Everything he does is done in his name. His "I" becomes totally relative to the "I" of Jesus. In the name of Christ, and most certainly not in his own, the apostle may perform acts of healing for the brethren, may help the "crippled" to rise again and take their path (cf. Acts 4:9-10). In Peter's case, the miracle that had just occurred makes this especially evident. And even the reference to what was said in the psalm is essential: "The stone which the builders rejected has become the corner stone" (Ps. 118[117]:22). Jesus was "rejected," but the Father favored him and put him as the foundation of the Temple of the New Covenant. Thus the apostle, like the priest, experiences in turn the Cross, and only through this can he become truly useful to the building of the Church. God loves to build his Church with people who, following Jesus, place their entire trust in God.

The Ascension

The historical character of the mystery of Christ's resurrection and ascension helps us to recognize and to understand the transcendent state of the Church, which is not born and does not live in order to compensate for the absence of the "invisible" Lord, but instead finds her raison d'être *and her mission in the permanent, though invisible, presence of Jesus, a presence that acts with the power of his Spirit. In other words, we are able to say that the Church does not play the role of preparing for the return of the "absent" Jesus, but, on the contrary, she lives and works in order to proclaim his "glorious presence" in a historical and existential way. Since the day of the Ascension, every Christian community progresses in its earthly itinerary toward the fulfillment of the messianic promises, strengthened by the Word of God and nourished by the Lord's Body and Blood.*

"You shall receive power when the Holy Spirit has come upon you; and you shall be my witnesses in Jerusalem and in all Judea and Samaria and to the end of the earth" (Acts 1:8). With these words, Jesus took his leave of the apostles, as we heard in the First Reading. Immediately afterwards the sacred author adds that "as they were looking on, he was lifted up, and a cloud took him out of their sight" (Acts 1:9). This is the mystery of the Ascension that we are celebrating today. In the passage from the Acts of the Apostles it is said first that Jesus was "lifted up" (v. 9) and then it says "taken up" (v. 11). The event is not described as a journey to on high but rather as an action of the power of God who introduces Jesus into the space of closeness to the Divine. The presence of the cloud that "took him out of their sight" (v. 9) recalls a very ancient image of Old Testament theology and integrates the account of the Ascension into the history of God with Israel, from the cloud of Sinai and above the tent of the Covenant in the desert, to the luminous cloud on the mountain of the Transfiguration. To present the Lord wrapped in clouds calls to mind once and for all the same mystery expressed in the symbolism of the phrase "seated at the right hand of God." In Christ ascended into heaven, the human being has entered into intimacy with God in a new and unheard-of way; we henceforth find room in God forever. "Heaven": the word does not indicate a place above the stars but something far more daring and sublime: it indicates Christ himself, the divine Person who welcomes humanity fully and forever, the One in whom God and man are inseparably united forever. The human's being in God — this is heaven.

Pentecost

Among all the feast days, Pentecost has a unique importance: it is on Pentecost that what Jesus himself announced as the goal of his entire earthly mission comes to fruition. While he was going up to Jerusalem he said to his disciples: "I came to set fire to the earth; and how I wish that it was already burning!" (Luke 12:49). These words find their clearest realization fifty days after the resurrection, on Pentecost, the ancient Jewish feast that became in the Church the feast par excellence of the Holy Spirit: "And there appeared to them tongues as of fire; they all were thus filled with the Holy Spirit" (Acts 2:3-4). The true fire, the Holy Spirit, was brought to the earth by Christ. He did not steal it from the gods, as did Prometheus in the Greek myth, but he became the mediator of the "gift of God" and he obtained it for us by the greatest act of love in history: his death on the Cross.

In today's solemnity, Scripture tells us how the community must be, how we must be to receive the Holy Spirit. In his account of Pentecost the sacred author says that the disciples "were together in the same place." This "place" is the Cenacle, the "upper room," where Jesus held the Last Supper with his disciples, where he appeared to them after his resurrection; the room that had become the "seat," so to speak, of the nascent Church (cf. Acts 1:13). Nevertheless, the intention in the Acts of the Apostles is more to indicate the interior attitude of the disciples than to insist on a physical place: "They all persevered in concord and prayer" (Acts 1:14). So, the concord of the disciples is the condition for the coming of the Holy Spirit; and prayer is the presupposition of concord. To indicate the Holy Spirit, the account in the Acts of the Apostles uses two great images, the image of the tempest and the image of fire. Clearly, St. Luke had in mind the theophany of Sinai, recounted in Exodus (19:16-19) and Deuteronomy (4:10–12:36). In the ancient world the tempest was seen as a sign of divine power, in whose presence man felt subjugated and terrified. But I would like to highlight another aspect: the tempest is described as a "strong driving wind," and this brings to mind the air that distinguishes our planet from others and permits us to live on it. What air is for biological life, the Holy Spirit is for the spiritual life.

Fire is the other image of the Holy Spirit that we find in the Acts of the Apostles. Taking control of the energies of the cosmos — "fire" — today human beings seem to claim themselves as gods and want to transform the world, excluding, putting aside, or simply rejecting the Creator of the universe. Man no longer wants to be the image of God but the image of himself; he declares himself autonomous, free, adult. Obviously that reveals an inauthentic relationship with God, the consequence of a false image that has been constructed of him, like the prodigal son in the Gospel parable who thought that he could find himself by distancing himself from the house of his father. In the hands of man in this condition, "fire" and its enormous possibilities become dangerous: they can destroy life and humanity itself, as history unfortunately shows.

Ordinary Time: After Pentecost

After the Easter season, which culminated in the feast of Pentecost, the liturgy foresees the following three solemnities of the Lord: the feast of the Most Holy Trinity, the feast of Corpus Christi, and, finally, the feast of the Sacred Heart of Jesus. Each of these liturgical feasts brings to light a perspective that enables us to embrace the entire scope of the mystery of the Christian faith: respectively, the reality of God as One and Triune, the sacrament of the Eucharist, and the divine and human center of the Person of Christ. These are in truth the various aspects of the one mystery of salvation, which, in a certain way, sums up the whole itinerary of Jesus' revelation, from the incarnation to the death and resurrection, up to the ascension and the gift of the Holy Spirit.

Feast of the Most Holy Trinity

Three Persons who are *one God* because the Father is love, the Son is love, the Spirit is love. God is wholly and only love: the purest, infinite, and eternal love. He does not live in splendid solitude but rather is an inexhaustible source of life that is ceaselessly given and communicated. To a certain extent we can perceive this by observing both the macro-universe: our earth, the planets, the stars, the galaxies; and the micro-universe: cells, atoms, elementary particles. The "name" of the Blessed Trinity is, in a certain sense, imprinted upon all things because all that exists, down to the last particle, is in relation; in this way we catch a glimpse of God as relationship and ultimately as Creator Love. All things derive from love, aspire to love, and move impelled by love, though naturally with varying degrees of awareness and freedom. "O Lord, our Lord, how majestic is your name in all the earth!" (Ps. 8:1) the psalmist exclaims. In speaking of the "name," the Bible refers to God himself, his truest identity. It is an identity that shines upon the whole of creation, in which all beings for the very fact that they exist and because of the "fabric" of which they are made point to a transcendent Principle, to eternal and infinite Life which is given, in a word, to Love.

Corpus Christi

For the Corpus Christi procession, the pope leads the people, who carry the blessed sacrament, through the streets of Rome, from the Basilica of St. John Lateran to the Basilica of Santa Maria Maggiore.

"This is my Body. . . . This is my Blood": These words that Jesus spoke at the Last Supper are repeated every time the eucharistic sacrifice is renewed. We have just heard them in Mark's Gospel, and they resonate with special power today on the solemnity of *Corpus Christi*. They lead us in spirit to the Upper Room; they make us relive the spiritual atmosphere of that night when, celebrating Easter with his followers, the Lord mystically anticipated the sacrifice that was to be consummated the following day on the Cross. The Institution of the Eucharist thus appears to us as an anticipation and acceptance, on Jesus' part, of his death. St. Ephrem the Syrian writes on this topic: during the Supper, Jesus sacrificed himself; on the Cross he was sacrificed by others (cf. *Hymn on the Crucifixion,* 3:1). *"This is my Blood."* Here the reference to the sacrificial language of Israel is clear. Jesus presents himself as the true and definitive sacrifice, in which was fulfilled the expiation of sins which, in the Old Testament rites, was never fully completed. This is followed by two other very important remarks. First of all, Jesus Christ says that his blood *"is poured out for many,"* with a comprehensible reference to the songs of the Servant of God that are found in the book of Isaiah (cf. ch. 53). With the addition *"blood of the Covenant,"* Jesus also makes clear that through his death the prophecy of the new Covenant is fulfilled, based on the fidelity and infinite love of the Son made man. An alliance that, therefore, is stronger than all humanity's sins.

The Sacred Heart of Jesus

"The Lord has received us into his heart — Suscepit nos Dominus in sinum et cor suum." *The Old Testament refers to*

the "heart of God" twenty-six times, which it presents as the or-
gan of his will. It is with respect to the heart of God that man is
judged. Because of the suffering that this heart has endured
for the sins of man, God decided to allow the flood; but he is
moved at the sight of human weakness, and he forgives. The
essential core of Christianity is expressed in the heart of Jesus.

On today's solemnity of the Sacred Heart of Jesus the
Church presents us this mystery for our contemplation: the
mystery of the heart of a God who feels compassion and
who bestows all his love upon humanity — a mysterious
love, which in the texts of the New Testament is revealed to
us as God's boundless and passionate love for humankind.
God does not lose heart in the face of ingratitude or rejec-
tion by the people he has chosen; rather, with infinite mercy
he sends his only-begotten Son into the world to take upon
himself the fate of a shattered love, so that by defeating the
power of evil and death he could restore to human beings
enslaved by sin their dignity as sons and daughters. But this
took place at great cost — the only-begotten Son of the Father was sacrificed on the Cross: "Having loved his own who
were in the world, he loved them to the end" (cf. John 13:1).

The symbol of this love that transcends death is his side, pierced by a spear. The Apostle John, an eyewitness, tells us: "One of the soldiers pierced his side with a spear, and at once there came out blood and water" (cf. John 19:34). In Christ the revolutionary "newness" of the gospel is completely revealed and given to us: the Love that saves us and even now makes us live in the eternity of God. As the Evangelist John writes: "God so loved the world that he gave his only Son, that whoever believes in him should not perish but have eternal life" (3:16). God's heart calls to our hearts, inviting us to come out of ourselves, to forsake our human certainties, to trust in him and, by following his example, to make ourselves a gift of unbounded love.

First Vespers on the Feast of St. Paul

What characterizes the letters of St. Paul is that they explain above all the mystery of Christ; they teach us the faith, always in reference to a particular place and situation.

The world is always in search of novelty because, rightly, it is always dissatisfied with concrete reality. Paul tells us: the world cannot be renewed without new people. Only if there are new people will there also be a new world, a renewed and better world. In the beginning is the renewal of the human being. This subsequently applies to every individual. Only if we ourselves become new does the world become new. This also means that it is not enough to adapt to the current situation. The apostle exhorts us to nonconformism. In our Letter [Romans] he says: we should not submit to the logic of our time. We shall return to this point, reflecting on the second text on which I wish to meditate with you this evening. The apostle's "no" is clear and also convincing for anyone who observes the "logic" of our world. But to become new: How can this be done? Are we really capable of it? With his words on becoming new, Paul alludes to his own conversion: to his encounter with the risen Christ, an encounter of which, in the second letter to the Corinthians he says: "If anyone is in Christ, he is in a new creation; the old has passed away; behold, the new has come" (5:17). This encounter with Christ was so overwhelming for him that he said of it: "I . . . died . . ." (Gal. 2:19; cf. Rom. 6). He became new, another, because he no longer lived for himself and by virtue of himself, but for Christ and in him. In the course of the years, however, he also saw that this process of renewal and transformation continues throughout life. We become new if we let ourselves be grasped and shaped by the new Man, Jesus Christ. He is the new Man par excellence. In him the new human existence became reality, and we can truly become new if we deliver ourselves into his hands and let ourselves be molded by him.

Saints Peter and Paul

This is the feast day of the Eternal City. On this occasion, the pope places the pallium on the metropolitan archbishops who were named over the course of the year.

Do we ourselves follow the teaching of the apostles who were the great founders? Do we really know them? The first letter of St. Peter is a salutation addressed from Rome to the whole of Christianity throughout the ages. It invites us to listen to the "teaching of the apostles," which directs us toward the path that leads to life.

———

"In your hearts reverence Christ as Lord. Always be prepared to make a defense to anyone who calls you to account for the hope that is in you" (1 Peter 3:15). Christian faith is hope. It paves the way to the future. And it is a hope that possesses reasonableness, a hope whose reason we can and must explain. Faith comes from the eternal Reason that entered our world and showed us the true God. Faith surpasses the capacity of our reason, just as love sees more than mere intelligence. But faith speaks to reason and in the dialectic confrontation can be a match for reason. It does not contradict it but keeps up with it and goes beyond it to introduce us into the greater Reason of God. As pastors of our time it is our task to be the first to understand the reason of faith. It is our task not to let it remain merely a tradition but to recognize it as a response to our questions. Faith demands our rational participation, which is deepened and purified in a sharing of love. It is one of our duties as pastors to penetrate faith with thought, to be able to show the reason for our hope within the debates of our time. Yet although it is so necessary, thought alone does not suffice. Just as speaking alone does not suffice. In his baptismal and eucharistic catechesis in chapter 2 of his second letter, Peter alludes to the Psalm used by the ancient Church in the context of communion, that is, to the verse that says: "O taste and see that the Lord is good!" (Ps. 34[33]:8; 1 Peter 2:3).

Tasting alone leads to seeing. Let us think of the disciples of Emmaus: it was only in convivial communion with Jesus, only in the breaking of the bread that their eyes were opened. Only in truly experienced communion with the Lord were they able to see. This applies to us all; over and above thinking and speaking, we need the experience of faith, the vital relationship with Jesus Christ. Faith must not remain theory: it must be life.

August 15: The Assumption

The whole of life is an ascent; the whole of life is meditation, obedience, trust and hope, even in the times of darkness. Man's life on earth is a path that constantly unfolds in the tension of the battle between the dragon and the woman, between good and evil. Such is the situation of human history: it is like a voyage on an often-stormy sea; Mary is the star who guides us toward her Son Jesus, and she gives us the hope that we need. Mary's "yes" was thus the gate through which God was able to enter into the world, to become man. Thus, Mary participates in a real and profound way in the mystery of the incarnation, which is the mystery of our salvation.

Today's solemnity crowns the series of important liturgical
celebrations in which we are called to contemplate the role
of the Blessed Virgin Mary in the history of salvation. Indeed, the Immaculate Conception, the Annunciation, the
Divine Motherhood, and the Assumption are the fundamental, interconnected milestones with which the Church ex-
alts and praises the glorious destiny of the Mother of God,
but in which we can also read our history. The mystery of
Mary's conception recalls the first page of the human event,
pointing out to us that in the divine plan of creation man
was to have had the purity and beauty of the Virgin Immaculate. This plan, jeopardized but not destroyed by sin,
through the incarnation of the Son of God, proclaimed and
brought into being in Mary, was recomposed and restored
to the free acceptance of the human being in faith. In Mary's
Assumption, we contemplate what we ourselves are called
to attain in the following of Christ the Lord and in obedience to his word, at the end of our earthly journey. The last
stage of the Mother of God's earthly pilgrimage invites us to
look at the manner in which she journeyed on toward the
goal of glorious eternity. And, lastly, the Assumption re-

minds us that Mary's life, like that of every Christian, is a journey of following — following Jesus — a journey that has a very precise destination, a future already marked out: the definitive victory over sin and death and full communion with God.

September 14: The Elevation of the Cross

The Virgin Mary, who believed in the word of the Lord, did not lose her faith in God when she saw her Son rejected, abused, and crucified. Rather she remained beside Jesus, suffering and praying, until the end. And she saw the radiant dawn of his resurrection. Let us learn from her to witness to our faith with a life of humble service, ready to personally pay the price of staying faithful to the gospel of love and truth, certain that nothing we do will be lost.

All Saints' Day

The solemnity of All Saints invites the pilgrim Church on earth to a foretaste of the everlasting feast in the community of heaven, and to revive our hope in eternal life. The Pantheon — one of the oldest and most famous of the Roman monuments — was dedicated to Christian worship and named after the Virgin Mary and all the Martyrs: *Sancta Maria ad Martyres.* The temple of all the pagan divinities was thus converted to commemorate all those who, as the book of Revelation says, "have come out of the great tribulations; they have washed their robes and made them white in the blood of the Lamb" (Rev. 7:14). Subsequently, the celebration of all the martyrs was extended to all the saints: "a great multitude which no man could number, from every nation, from all tribes and peoples and tongues" (Rev. 7:9) according to St. John. How beautiful and comforting is the communion of saints! It is a reality that instills a different dimension into our whole life. We are never alone! We are part of a spiritual "company" where profound solidarity reigns: the good of each one is for the benefit of everyone, and vice versa; common happiness shines on every individual. It is a mystery that in some measure we can already experience in this world, in the family, in friendship, and especially in the spiritual community of the Church.

All Souls' Day

I would like to invite you to live this annual celebration in keeping with a genuine Christian spirit, that is, in the light that proceeds from the Paschal Mystery. Christ has died and risen and has opened to us the way to the house of the Father, the Kingdom of life and peace. He who follows Jesus in this life is received where he has preceded us. Therefore, while we visit cemeteries, let us remember that there, in the tombs, only the mortal remains of our loved ones rest, while awaiting the final resurrection. Their souls — as Scripture says — already "are in the hand of God" (Wisdom 3:1). Hence, the most appropriate and effective way to honor them is to pray for them, offering acts of faith, hope, and charity. In union with the eucharistic sacrifice, we can intercede for their eternal salvation, and experience the most profound communion while waiting to be reunited again, to enjoy forever the love that created us and redeemed us.

Christ the King

The final Sunday of the liturgical year, the solemnity of Jesus Christ, King of the universe, has deep roots in the Bible and the theological tradition.

———

The title "King," designating Jesus, is very important in the Gospels and makes possible a complete interpretation of the figure of Jesus and of his mission of salvation. In this regard a progression can be noted: it starts with the expression "King of Israel" and extends to that of universal King, Lord of the cosmos and of history, thus exceeding by far the expectations of the Jewish people. It is yet again the mystery of Jesus Christ's death and resurrection that lies at the heart of this process of the revelation of his kingship. When Jesus is hung on the Cross, the priests, scribes, and elders mock him saying: "He is the King of Israel; let him come down now from the cross, and we will believe in him" (Matt. 27:42). In fact, it is precisely as the Son of God that Jesus freely gives himself up to his Passion. The Cross is the paradoxical sign of his kingship, which consists in the loving will of God the Father in response to the disobedience of sin. It is in the very

offering of himself in the sacrifice of expiation that Jesus becomes King of the universe, as he himself was to declare
when he appeared to the apostles after the resurrection: "All
authority in heaven and on earth has been given to me"
(Matt. 28:18).

Sources

All translations of texts from Benedict XVI are © Libreria Editrice Vaticana.

First Vespers of Advent
  Homily, 28 November 2009

First Sunday of Advent
  Angelus, 29 November 2009

December 8: The Immaculate Conception,
the Second Sunday of Advent
  Angelus, 8 December 2009

December 12: Our Lady of Guadalupe
  Homily, 12 December 2011

Sources

Third Sunday of Advent
Angelus, 13 December 2009

Fourth Sunday of Advent
Angelus, 20 December 2009

December 24, Christmas Eve
Homily, 25 December 2008

December 25, Christmas
Homily, 11 January 2009

December 26, St. Stephen Martyr
Angelus, 26 December 2008

The Feast of the Holy Family
Angelus, 28 December 2008

December 31, Recitation of the *Te Deum* in Thanksgiving
Homily, 31 December 2008

January 1: Solemnity of Mary, Mother of God
Homily, 1 January 2009

January 6: Epiphany of the Lord
Homily, 6 January 2009

Sources

January 13: Baptism of the Lord
  Homily, 11 January 2009

January 25: The Conversion of St. Paul
  Angelus, 25 June 2009 and Homily 25 June 2009

February 2: The Presentation of the Lord at the Temple
(Candlemass)
  Address after Mass, 2 February 2009

February 11: The Solemnity of the Blessed Virgin of Lourdes
  Address after Mass, 11 February 2009

Ash Wednesday
  Homily, 25 February 2009

First Sunday of Lent
  Angelus, 1 March 2009

Second Sunday of Lent
  Angelus, 8 March 2009

February 22: The Feast of the Chair of Peter
  Angelus, 22 February 2009

Annunciation
  Angelus, 25 March 2007

SOURCES

Third Sunday of Lent
Angelus, 24 February 2008

Fourth Sunday of Lent
Angelus, 2 March 2008

March 19: The Solemnity of St. Joseph
Homily, 19 March 2009

Fifth Sunday of Lent
Angelus, 9 March 2008

Palm Sunday
Homily, 5 April 2009

Holy Thursday, Chrism Mass
Homily, 9 April 2009

Mass of the Lord's Supper
Audience, 8 April 2009

Good Friday
Audience, 8 April 2009

Easter
Urbi et Orbi, *Easter 2009*

Sources

Easter Monday
   Audience, 15 April 2009

Divine Mercy Sunday
   Regina Coeli, *19 April 2009*

Third Sunday of Easter
   Homily, 26 April 2009

Fourth Sunday of Easter, or Good Shepherd Sunday
   Homily, 3 May 2009

The Ascension
   Homily, 24 May 2009

Pentecost
   Homily, 31 May 2009

Feast of the Holy Trinity
   Homily, 6 June 2009

Corpus Christi
   Homily, 11 June 2009

The Sacred Heart of Jesus
   Homily, 19 June 2009

SOURCES

First Vespers on the Feast of St. Paul
  Homily, 28 June 2009

Sts. Peter and Paul
  Homily, 29 June 2009

August 15: The Assumption
  Homily, 15 August 2009

September 14: The Elevation of the Cross
  Angelus, 13 September 2009

All Saints' Day
  Angelus, 1 November 2009

All Souls' Day
  Angelus, 2 November 2009

Christ the King
  Angelus, 22 November 2009